Preface
≈

Richard Rudisill, Curator of Photographic History, Museum of New Mexico

The Historical Society of New Mexico began collecting pictures soon after its founding in 1859 with catalogue accessions including "Two Photographic views of the Washington Aqueduct" and "An ambrotype of José Calixto Borrego the Mexican dwarf." Although these initial pieces vanished in the disruption of the Civil War, the rebirth of the society in 1880 began steady growth of a collection which was assigned to the Museum of New Mexico in 1977. Since then, overall holdings have reached to half a million items. Subject-matter filing allows researchers to look as much as fourteen decades into New Mexico's past, to view buildings and spaces of Santa Fe or various pueblos, to see past dress styles or work actions, to meet face-to-face the people of earlier days, and to perceive the large and small changes in life otherwise unreachable or forgotten.

    Many of these views were made by professionals, upon request or for their own reasons, as entertainment or postcards, for publication or sale. A great number came about simply as personal responses to family events and daily lives that elicited a wish to keep bits of them permanent or to share details with others. A remarkable aspect of the entire collection is that drastic changes in physical circumstances have not been matched by equal shift in the attitudes people hold about why they make pictures or why they enjoy them. Methods of scholarship or social conditions may fluctuate, but most people go on wanting to see how they or their predecessors have appeared and what remains recognizable from a time before. Nostalgia weighs as much as scholarship in such scales of appreciation.

Through its later history, New Mexico stayed current with general photographic practice. By the 1860s and '70s, a few of the studios in the territory were capable of issuing the popular stereoscopic views or producing sunlight enlargements equal with work from "the States." With the advent of the railroad and greater attention from anthropologists, artists, tourists, and traders, the materials and techniques of contemporary eastern work were to be had in Santa Fe or Las Vegas or New Albuquerque, and several major people worked or lived in the region. Ben Wittick, John K. Hillers, Willilam Henry Jackson, and Dana B. Chase were among them.

In the thirty years before World War I, Charles Lummis made hundreds of iron-base blueprints of Indian life, Adam Clark Vroman wrought images in platinum, Aaron Craycraft lugged an 8"x10" view camera into Frijoles Canyon and introduced Dr. Edgar Hewett (archaeologist and founder of the Museum of New Mexico) to the now-famous Tyuonyi Ruins, and Jesse Nusbaum pictured the architecture and rural details of northern New Mexico before recording the new museum's clearing of the Maya site of Quirigua in Guatemala and then going on to carry Pueblo-style structures into the 1915 Panama-California Exposition in San Diego. Then, and later, T. Harmon Parkhurst, H.F. Robinson, and Wesley Bradfield created arrays of negatives reflecting changes in town and Pueblo Indian life. Throughout all that time, amateurs were busy recording whatever the professionals missed to a degree that allows today's Museum of New Mexico Photo Archives to show the richly alive visual heritage of New Mexico.

The Postcard Archive Series

From **Villages of the Rio Grande**. © 1994 MUSEUM OF NEW MEXICO PRESS, SANTA FE

Winnowing beans, Rio Arriba County, New Mexico, ca. 1920. MNM 31499.

The Postcard Archive Series

From **Villages of the Rio Grande**, © 1994 MUSEUM OF NEW MEXICO PRESS, SANTA FE

Main street, Tierra Amarilla, New Mexico, ca. 1890.

The **Postcard Archive Series**

From **Villages of the Rio Grande,** © 1994 MUSEUM OF NEW MEXICO PRESS, SANTA FE

Spanish-American women replastering an adobe house. This is done once a year. Chamisal, NM, 1940. Photo by Russell Lee, courtesy Library of Congress.

The Postcard Archive Series

From **Villages of the Rio Grande**, © 1994 MUSEUM OF NEW MEXICO PRESS, SANTA FE

Threshing, New Mexico, ca. 1920. MNM 27975.

The Postcard Archive Series

From **Villages of the Rio Grande**, © 1994 MUSEUM OF NEW MEXICO PRESS, SANTA FE

Farmstead of a Spanish-American farmer.
Chamisal, New Mexico, 1940. Photo by
Russell Lee, courtesy Library of Congress.

The Postcard Archive Series

From ***Villages of the Rio Grande***, © 1994 MUSEUM OF NEW MEXICO PRESS, SANTA FE

Procession of Spanish-American Catholics
to honor a saint. Peñasco, New Mexico, 1940.
Photo by Russell Lee, courtesy Library of Congress.

The Postcard Archive Series

From **Villages of the Rio Grande**, © 1994 MUSEUM OF NEW MEXICO PRESS, SANTA FE

Front yard of a Spanish-American home
near Questa, New Mexico, 1940. Photo by
Russell Lee, courtesy Library of Congress.

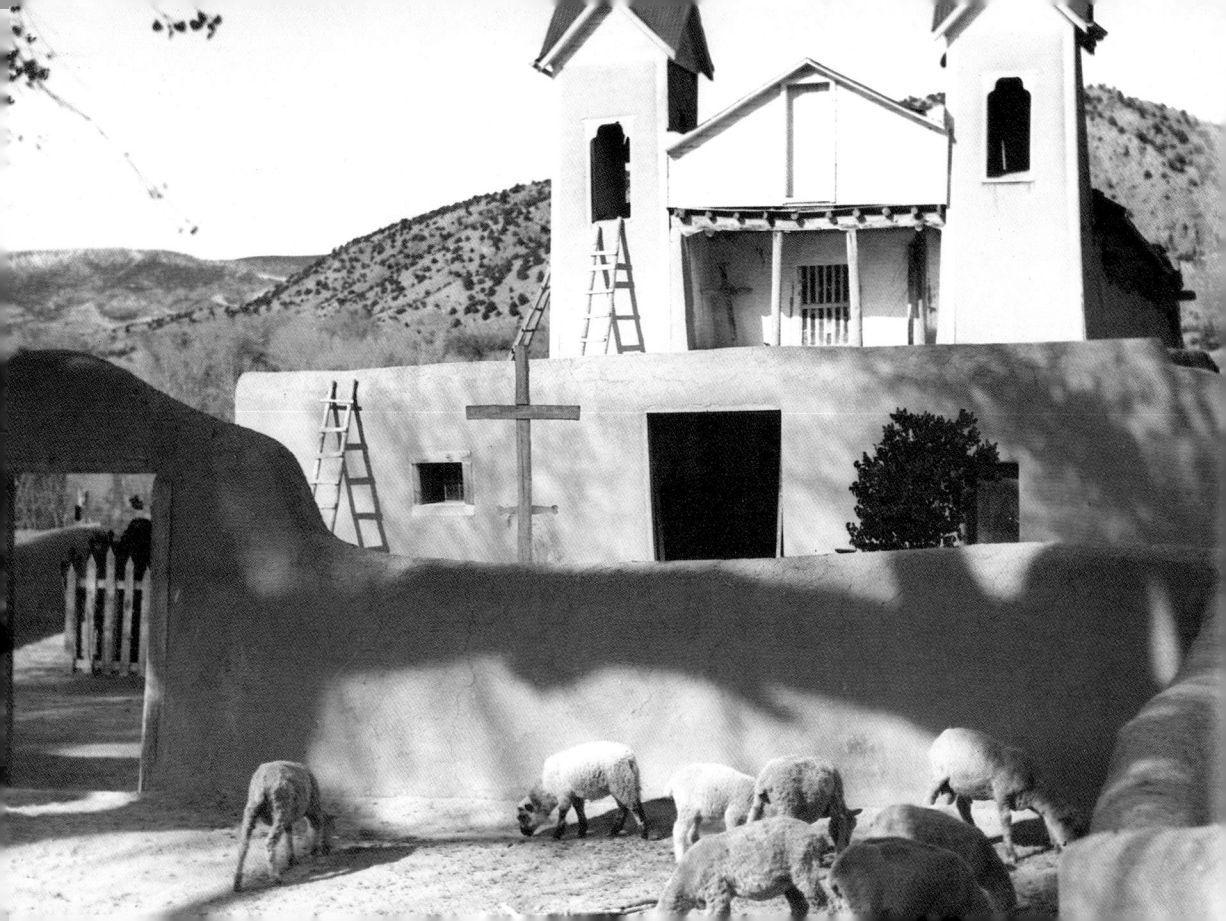

The Postcard Archive Series

From **Villages of the Rio Grande**. © 1994 MUSEUM OF NEW MEXICO PRESS, SANTA FE

Sheep grazing outside the courtyard of the Santuario de Chimayó, New Mexico, ca. 1935. Photo by T. Harmon Parkhurst. MNM 8894.

≈

The Postcard Archive Series

≈

From **Villages of the Rio Grande**. © 1994 MUSEUM OF NEW MEXICO PRESS, SANTA FE

Córdova, New Mexico, woodcarver José Dolores López with his bulto of the Blessed Virgin Mary, ca. 1935. Photo by T. Harmon Parkhurst. MNM 94470.

≈

The Postcard Archive Series

≈

From **Villages of the Rio Grande**, © 1994 MUSEUM OF NEW MEXICO PRESS, SANTA FE

Religious procession, Santuario de Chimayó, New Mexico, 1910. Photo by Jesse L. Nusbaum. MNM 14379.

The
Postcard
Archive
Series

From **Villages of the Rio Grande**. © 1994 MUSEUM OF NEW MEXICO PRESS, SANTA FE

Family husking corn, northern New Mexico, ca. 1905. Photo by Edward Andrews. MNM 71218.

The Postcard Archive Series

From **Villages of the Rio Grande**, © 1994 MUSEUM OF NEW MEXICO PRESS, SANTA FE

Spanish-American couple preparing fruit for canning. Chamisal, New Mexico, 1940. Photo by Russell Lee, courtesy Library of Congress.

≈

The Postcard Archive Series

≈

From **Villages of the Rio Grande**, © 1994 MUSEUM OF NEW MEXICO PRESS, SANTA FE

The mail comes to town in this light wagon. Peñasco, New Mexico, 1940. Photo by Russell Lee, courtesy Library of Congress.

≈

The
Postcard
Archive
Series

≈

From **Villages of the Rio Grande**, © 1994 MUSEUM OF NEW MEXICO PRESS, SANTA FE

Threshing wheat with goats, Córdova, New Mexico, ca. 1935. Photo by T. Harmon Parkhurst. MNM 9059.

≈

The Postcard Archive Series

≈

From **Villages of the Rio Grande**. 1994 MUSEUM OF NEW MEXICO PRESS, SANTA FE

Drying chile, Rio Arriba County, NM, ca. 1920. MNM 31507.

The Postcard Archive Series

From **Villages of the Rio Grande,** © 1994 MUSEUM OF NEW MEXICO PRESS, SANTA FE

Santa Fe sheriff Milo Martinez and his wife, ca. 1890. Photo by James N. Furlong. MNM 12114.

≈

The Postcard Archive Series

≈

From **Villages of the Rio Grande**. © 1994 MUSEUM OF NEW MEXICO PRESS, SANTA FE

A descanso, a shrine or resting place, on a hillside in Truchas, New Mexico, ca. 1935. Photo by T. Harmon Parkhurst. MNM 11592.

≈

The Postcard Archive Series

≈

From **Villages of the Rio Grande.** © 1994 MUSEUM OF NEW MEXICO PRESS, SANTA FE

Hispanic wedding group in Santa Fe, New Mexico, 1912. Photo by Jesse L. Nusbaum. MNM 61817

The Postcard Archive Series

From **Villages of the Rio Grande**, © 1994 MUSEUM OF NEW MEXICO PRESS, SANTA FE

Weaver in the Gans Store, Chimayó, New Mexico, ca. 1935. Photo by T. Harmon Parkhurst. MNM 6918.

The Postcard Archive Series

From ***Villages of the Rio Grande***. © 1994 MUSEUM OF NEW MEXICO PRESS, SANTA FE

Spanish-American farmers, the Domínguez family, loading a mower onto a truck. Chamisal, NM, 1940. Photo by Russell Lee, courtesy Library of Congress.

The Postcard Archive Series

From **Villages of the Rio Grande**. © 1994 MUSEUM OF NEW MEXICO PRESS, SANTA FE

Sitting room at the Jésus Baca Ranch in northern NM, ca. 1935. Photo by T. Harmon Parkhurst. MNM 88083.

The Postcard Archive Series

From **Villages of the Rio Grande.** © 1994 MUSEUM OF NEW MEXICO PRESS, SANTA FE

Chimayó weaver José Ortega creating a special design for the Elks Lodge of Santa Fe, 1959. Photo by E.P. Haddon and Mary Branham. MNM 127464.

The Postcard Archive Series

From **Villages of the Rio Grande**. © 1994 MUSEUM OF NEW MEXICO PRESS, SANTA FE

Orchestra playing in front of a hall to attract a crowd to the show. Peñasco, New Mexico, 1940. Photo by Russell Lee, courtesy Library of Congress.

The Postcard Archive Series

From **Villages of the Rio Grande**, © 1994 MUSEUM OF NEW MEXICO PRESS, SANTA FE

Spanish-American girls, Chamisal, New Mexico, 1940.
Photo by Russell Lee, courtesy Library of Congress.

The Postcard Archive Series

From **Villages of the Rio Grande**, © 1994 MUSEUM OF NEW MEXICO PRESS, SANTA FE

Formal wedding portrait of Mrs. Enrique Salazar, ca. 1890. MNM 7637.

From **Villages of the Rio Grande,** © 1994 MUSEUM OF NEW MEXICO PRESS, SANTA FE

Wedding procession leaving church, Córdova, New Mexico, 1939. Photo by B. Brixner. MNM 12034.

≈

The Postcard Archive Series

≈

From **Villages of the Rio Grande,** © 1994 MUSEUM OF NEW MEXICO PRESS, SANTA FE

Hispanic woman baking bread in a traditional outdoor oven. Santa Fe, New Mexico, ca. 1898. Photo by Christian G. Kaadt. MNM 69106.

≈

The Postcard Archive Series

≈

From **Villages of the Rio Grande**, © 1994 MUSEUM OF NEW MEXICO PRESS, SANTA FE

Spanish-American woman and baby in a flower garden. Chamisal, New Mexico, 1940. Photo by Russell Lee, courtesy Library of Congress.

≈

The
Postcard
Archive
Series

≈

From **Villages of the Rio Grande**, © 1994 MUSEUM OF NEW MEXICO PRESS, SANTA FE

The village of Las Trampas, founded in 1760, with the church in the center of town. Photo by Jesse L. Nusbaum, 1912. MNM 36466.

The Postcard Archive Series

From **Villages of the Rio Grande**. © 1994 MUSEUM OF NEW MEXICO PRESS, SANTA FE

Spanish-American farmer and his daughter seated on a couch built by his son at school. Chamisal, NM, 1940. Photo by Russell Lee, courtesy Library of Congress.